SCRAP ART FUN

Make DECOR AND MORE from the JUNK DRAWER

by Tamara JM Peterson
and Ruthie Van Oosbree

CAPSTONE PRESS
a capstone imprint

Dabble Lab is published by Capstone Press, an imprint of Capstone.
1710 Roe Crest Drive, North Mankato, Minnesota 56003
capstonepub.com

Copyright © 2024 by Capstone. All rights reserved. No part of this publication may be reproduced in whole or in part, or stored in a retrieval system, or transmitted in any form or by any means, electronic, mechanical, photocopying, recording, or otherwise, without written permission of the publisher.

Library of Congress Cataloging-in-Publication Data is available on the Library of Congress website.
ISBN: 9781669040064 (hardcover)
ISBN: 9781669040026 (ebook PDF)

Summary: Get inspired to sculpt cool decorations and practical pieces from everyday metal objects and junk drawer finds. You might build a handy hanger from old knobs or turn an empty tin into a planter. Organize and decorate your space in style with scrap metal art!

Image Credits
iStockphoto: Firuz Mukhtarov, 5 (epoxy), Lebazele, 5 (spray paint), SanerG, 5 (junk drawer, middle), sarahdoow, 5 (junk drawer, bottom), triffitt, 5 (junk drawer, top); Mighty Media, Inc.: project photos, supplies; Shutterstock Images: artdee2554, 18 (cat & dog), John M Ford, 7 (bottom), Konstantin Zubarev, 18 (texture in frame), PiercarloAbate, 7 (top left), PT Hamilton, 7 (top right), vitec, 5 (soda cans), Victor FlowerFly, 7 (middle), VitaArtUA, 4 (washers)

Design Elements
Shutterstock Images: mxbfilms, 32 pixels

Editorial Credits
Editor: Liz Salzmann
Designers: Sarah DeYoung and Tamara JM Peterson

All internet sites appearing in back matter were available and accurate when this book was sent to press.

The publisher and the author shall not be liable for any damages allegedly arising from the information in this book, and they specifically disclaim any liability from the use or application of any of the contents of this book.

Table of Contents

Heap to Handy 4
Basic Supplies 5
Smart Junk Art 5
Sourcing Scraps 6
Junk Art Inspiration 7

COZY CANDLEHOLDERS 8
BOWL O' BITS 10
RUSTIC RACK 12
SMARTPHONE SPEAKER 14
CAP COASTERS 16
FRENZIED FRAMES 18
UPCYCLED ACCESSORY 20
LOCKER CHANDELIER 22
SPARKLING LAMPSHADE 24
PUNCHY PLANTERS 28

Read More 32
Internet Sites 32
About the Authors 32

HEAP TO HANDY

With a few simple tools and some imagination, you can turn scrap metal and junk drawer treasures into all sorts of cool decorations and useful stuff! Look around for old, unwanted supplies. Then get creative! Transform them into beautiful, useful, and practical decor and more.

Build scrappy planters with old tins, unwanted jewelry, and bells.

Look for cans in your recycling bin. Then craft beautiful candleholders to light your way!

Gather metal bits and pieces to decorate a bowl.

Crafting with discarded junk has never been more fun—or functional!

BASIC SUPPLIES

SMART JUNK ART
Follow these tips to make your handy crafts a success!

Get Ready. Find all your materials and supplies. Read through the instructions carefully before starting a project. Cover your work surface to protect it from messes.

Scrap Safely. Ask an adult for help using hot or sharp tools. Never cut metal or use a hammer without adult supervision.

Ask First. They may be called junk drawers, but that doesn't mean everything in them is trash! Before you start crafting, get permission to use any supplies you find.

Keep It Clean. Tidy up after you're done crafting. Put supplies back where you found them. Clean up your workspace.

SOURCING SCRAPS

Finding the perfect junk for your project can be tricky. But don't rush to the store to buy supplies! Here are some ways to find cool materials for your decor and more.

Look in the recycling bin and junk drawer first. Ask an adult for suggestions of other places you could look. You might even ask friends and neighbors if they have things you could use.

Find alternatives. Most materials used in this book can be substituted with something else. If you're missing something, ask yourself what items you do have that could work instead.

Be on the lookout. Plan your crafts in advance. Then keep an eye out for items that could work for the project and collect them over time. You may be surprised at the useful bits and pieces you save that otherwise would have been thrown out!

Seek advice. Ask a friend or family member for ideas. They may think of substitutes for items you need. Don't be afraid to think outside the box—or the junk drawer!

If you decide you need to purchase supplies, start at a thrift store or surplus store. One person's trash may just be your scrap art treasure!

JUNK ART INSPIRATION

Junk art is a type of found art. Found art artists use everyday items to create art, such as sculptures or collages. Junk art artists do the same thing, but they focus on unwanted or discarded items. Artists have been creating found and junk art for more than a century. Get inspired by some cool pieces of junk art!

The Vollis Simpson Whirligig Park in Wilson, North Carolina, features many wind-powered structures. Vollis Simpson, a farm machinery repairman, made them out of parts he salvaged before his retirement.

The Cathedral of Junk in Austin, Texas, is a structure built by Vince Hannemann. He used more than 60 tons (54.4 tonnes) of junk, such as kitchen utensils, bicycle parts, and more.

Zimbabwean sculptor Tuckson Muvezwa's scrap metal sculptures were displayed on the grounds of Château de Gruyères in Switzerland.

Dr. Evermor's Forevertron in Sauk County, Wisconsin, is one of the largest scrap metal sculptures in the world. It is 50 feet (15.2 meters) high and 120 feet (36.5 m) wide, and it weighs 300 tons (272 t).

Cozy Candleholders

Tuck tealights into these scrappy candleholders. They're the perfect way to light up a cozy nook or cast a warm glow over a table!

MATERIALS

short tin cans

colored tape

junk drawer items, such as old chains and a metal ring

school glue

paintbrush

glitter

battery-operated tealights

1. Decorate the outside of the cans with colored tape.

2. Tape the end of a chain to the bottom of each can.

3. Connect the other ends of the chains to a metal ring.

4. Brush the bottom of each tin can with glue. Sprinkle glitter on the glue. Let the glue dry. Then dump out any loose glitter.

5. Hang the cans on the wall using the metal ring.

6. Turn on the tealights and set one in each can. Sit back and watch them sparkle!

Junk Art Tip

Instead of simple chains, look for broken necklaces, especially ones with beads on the chain.

Bowl o' Bits

Gather metal bits that are collecting dust and turn them into a unique and practical work of art. Keep jewelry or trinkets in this eye-catching bowl!

MATERIALS

plastic plate

plastic wrap

container to use as a mold

paper towel

tape

epoxy

metal bits, such as washers

junk drawer items, such as broken jewelry

unwanted stuff, such as a candlestick (optional)

1. Cover the plate with plastic wrap. Cover the mold with a paper towel and then plastic wrap. Use tape to hold the plastic wrap in place. Set the mold upside down on the plate.

2. Cover the mold with epoxy. Press as many washers as possible into the epoxy.

3. Press an old jewelry chain around the base of the mold. This will form the bowl's rim.

4. Use tape to help hold the pieces in place. Let the epoxy set overnight.

5. Remove the tape. Cover the bowl with epoxy and add more washers. Try not to place them directly over the other washers. Vary the arrangement. Let the epoxy set overnight.

6. Remove the bowl from the mold. Peel away the plastic wrap.

7. If you want your bowl to have a stem, glue it to a candlestick!

Rustic Rack

A simple hanger for keys, sweatshirts, bags, and more can help you stay organized. Craft this cool rack with a variety of spare knobs!

MATERIALS

piece of old wood

pencil

ruler

drill (with adult help)

junk drawer items, such as knobs, drawer pulls, and metal rings

screwdriver

3. Screw each of the knobs into the drilled holes on the board.

4. Attach two metal rings or drawer pulls with rings above the knobs. The rings should stick out past the top edge of the wood.

5. Use the rings to hang your rustic rack in a handy spot!

1. Make a mark on the wood where you want to put each knob. Use a ruler to make sure the marks are spaced evenly in a straight line.

2. Have an adult help you drill a hole at each mark.

Junk Art Tip

Look in your junk drawer for flat objects that could go under the knobs to add extra decoration.

Smartphone Speaker

This junk metal speaker lets you listen to music without breaking the bank. Decorate your speaker to reflect your unique style!

MATERIALS

smartphone

cardboard tube

pencil

craft knife

unwanted stuff, such as a metal cone and a metal disc

ruler

colored tape

hot glue gun

metal bits, such as nuts

1. Set the bottom edge of your phone on the tube. Trace around it in pencil. Cut along the lines with a craft knife.

2. Trace the small end of the cone on the tube 1 inch (2.5 cm) below the phone slot. Cut out the circle.

3. Cover the tube with colored tape.

4. Glue the tube to the metal disc so the phone slot faces up. Line the cone up with the hole cut in step 2. Glue the cone in place.

5. Glue nuts or other metal bits around the edges of the cone and tube for decoration.

6. Set your phone in the slot, turn on the music, and have a dance party!

Junk Art Tip

The best pieces can come from items you no longer use. In this case, the cone and the metal disc came from an old solar light.

Cap Coasters

Everyone can use more coasters! These bottle cap coasters protect surfaces and give you a cool spot to place your drink.

MATERIALS

cork sheet

junk drawer items, such as bottle caps

hot glue gun

scissors

3. Cut the cork sheet around the the bottle caps.

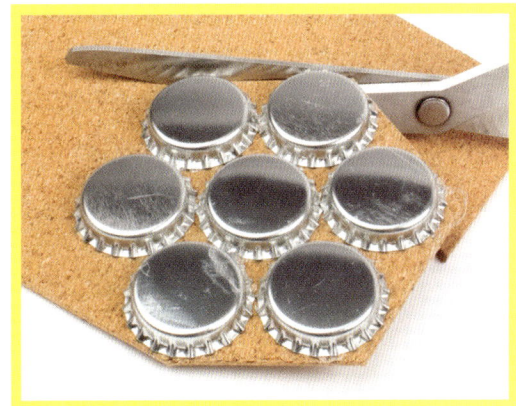

1. Arrange the bottle caps on the cork sheet. Try different shapes until you find one you like.

4. Repeat steps 1 through 3 to make more coasters. Share them with friends and family!

2. Glue the bottle caps in place.

Junk Art Tip

Try using more bottle caps to make a larger coaster to hold a hot pot or a platter.

Frenzied Frames

Give plain old picture frames a much-needed update with metal bits! Create a whole set to display your favorite photos or artwork.

MATERIALS

picture frame

metal bits, such as screws, washers, bolts, and gears

junk drawer items, such as bells and jewels

unwanted stuff, such as a valve handle and drawer pull

hot glue gun or epoxy

photos or artwork

2. Glue each piece onto the frame.

3. Repeat steps 1 and 2 to decorate more frames.

4. Pick out some photos or artwork to display in the frames and hang them up for everyone to see!

1. Arrange metal bits, junk drawer items, and unwanted stuff on the picture frame. You may need to take old items apart to get the pieces you want. Try different combinations until you like the way the frame looks.

Junk Art Tip

Include clusters of small, interesting pieces that stick out past the edge of the frame.

Upcycled Accessory

Make a fashion statement with scrap art! String soda can tabs onto colorful elastic for a unique and stylish bracelet.

MATERIALS

soda can tabs

pliers

metal file

junk drawer items, such as elastic and a necklace clasp

scissors

tape

1. Use pliers and a metal file to remove any sharp corners from the soda can tabs.

2. Arrange the tabs in the order you want them to go on the bracelet.

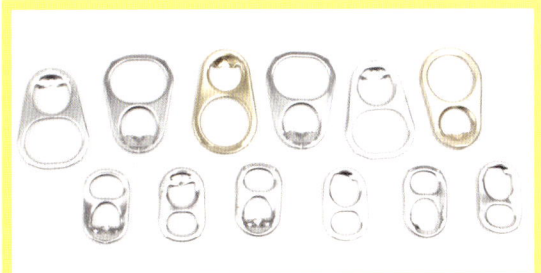

3. Cut two pieces of elastic that can wrap loosely around your wrist with a little extra. Tape the ends to a flat sturdy surface.

4. String the soda can tabs on the elastic. Try a few different ways of stringing them to decide what looks best. Push the tabs tightly together.

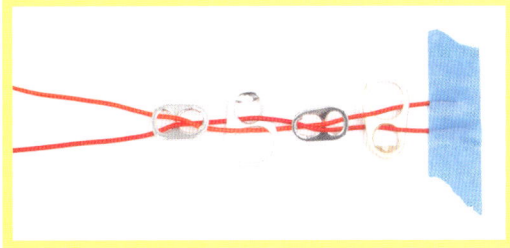

5. Weave more pieces of elastic through the soda can tabs if you'd like.

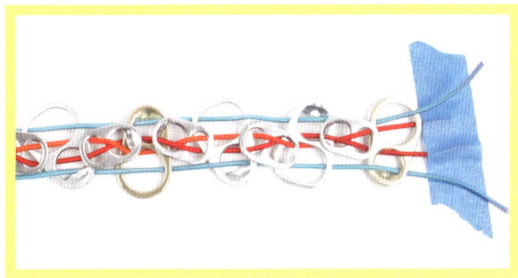

6. When you are done adding tabs and elastic, tie the elastic together at each end. Then tie each end to one half of an old necklace clasp. Cut off any extra elastic.

7. Wear your bracelet or give it to a friend or family member!

21

Locker Chandelier

Glam up your locker with leftover beads or crystals! String them together and glue them to a jar lid for a fantastic way to add sparkle to your school life.

MATERIALS

unwanted stuff, such as crystals or beads

junk drawer items, such as metal jump rings, wire, a jar lid, and a magnet

pliers

hot glue gun

1. Arrange the crystals in rows. Make a row for each strand you want to make.

2. Use pliers to attach the crystals in each row together with jump rings or wire.

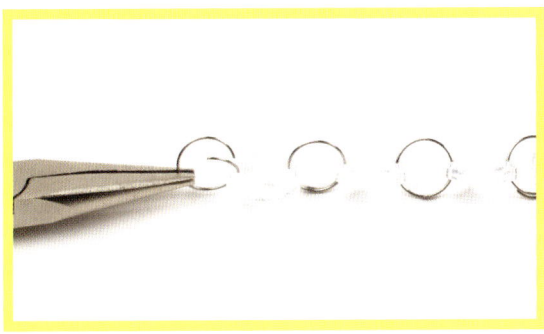

3. Glue the end of each strand inside the edge of the lid. Space the strands evenly around the lid.

4. Glue one longer strand to the middle of the lid.

5. Glue a magnet to the top of the lid.

6. Use the magnet to hang the chandelier in your locker. Enjoy the shiny crystals every time you open your locker!

Sparkling Lampshade

Use wires to craft your own custom lampshade. Then cover it with metal bits that catch the light!

MATERIALS

unwanted stuff, such as wreath forms, metal stakes, and a lamp base

pliers

electrical tape

metal screen

tin snips

junk drawer items, such as old keys and thin wire

decorative tape

metal bits, such as jump rings

1. Attach three metal stakes between two wreath forms. Space the stakes evenly. Use pliers to bend the ends of the stakes around the forms. This is the lampshade's frame.

2. Attach one end of three more stakes to the top of the frame. Tape the other ends of the stakes together. You will attach them to the lamp base later.

3. Cut a rectangle out of the metal screen. Make it long and wide enough to cover the entire frame.

4. Use thin wire to attach the screen to the top of the frame and to the vertical stakes.

Junk Art Tip

If you have an old lampshade, you can use it as a frame. Remove the fabric and put a screen on the frame. Or just attach the keys directly to the lampshade fabric.

Project continues on the next page.

5. Use more thin wire to attach the screen to the bottom of the frame.

6. Cover the top and bottom of the lampshade with decorative tape.

7. Spread the keys out on your work surface. Arrange them in the order you would like to hang them on the shade.

8. Put a key on a jump ring. Attach the jump ring to the screen. Use pliers to close the jump ring.

Junk Art Tip

If you don't have jump rings, you can make rings out of old wire. Wrap the wire a few times around the handle of a wooden spoon. Slide the wire off the handle and cut a straight line along the coil.

9. Repeat step 8 to attach the remaining keys to the screen. Add more decorative tape if you'd like.

10. Remove the tape that is holding the ends of the stakes inside the shade together.

11. Have a helper hold the lampshade over the lamp base. Use electrical tape to attach the ends of the stakes to the top of the lamp base. Be sure to use enough tape to hold the lampshade securely.

12. Turn on your lamp and watch the old keys sparkle!

Junk Art Tip

Do you need more keys? Try asking the person who cuts keys at a hardware store if they have any extras.

Punchy Planters

Turn simple tins into funky decorative planters with the help of some scrap metal! Bells and fun jewelry add personality and sparkle to your upcycled pots.

MATERIALS

metal tins without lids

paint and paintbrush

colored tape

junk drawer items, such as wire and bells

scrap wood

hammer and nail

metal bits, such as bolts

unwanted stuff, such as old jewelry and wire fencing

coffee filters

dirt

plant

1. Cover any parts of the tin you don't want to show with paint or colored tape.

2. Choose junk drawer items to decorate the tin. Take apart or reassemble the pieces however you would like to use them.

3. Set the tin on its side on scrap wood. Hammer a nail through the tin near the top edge. Remove the nail and turn the tin over. Hammer the nail through the opposite side. You'll attach the planter's hanger through these holes.

Project continues on the next page.

4. Use the hammer and nail to make a hole in the bottom of the tin. This is to let water drain out, and to attach a bell to.

5. Glue the junk drawer pieces to the tin. Add wire fencing or other decorations if you'd like.

6. Add a hanger. You could use a row of links cut from wire fencing or an old necklace. Attach the ends to the holes in the top of the tin.

7. Wrap a piece of old wire around a bolt.

Junk Art Tip

If you don't have tins or old jewelry lying around, try your local thrift store. You can often find great junk drawer items for craft projects there.

8. Put the bolt in the tin and thread the wire through the hole in the bottom. Attach a bell or other decoration to the wire.

9. Place a coffee filter in the planter. This will help keep the dirt from draining through the hole in the bottom.

10. Fill the coffee filter with dirt.

11. Add a plant to the dirt.

12. Repeat steps 1 through 11 to make more planters.

13. Hang the planters in a sunny spot. Water the plants lightly every few days. Watch your plants grow!

31

READ MORE

Borgert-Spaniol, Megan. *Mini Projects to Style Your Space*. North Mankato, MN: Capstone Press, 2023.

Morin, Marcy, and Heidi E. Thompson. *Eco-Crafts: 40 Fun Earth-Friendly Projects*. North Mankato, MN: Capstone Press, 2022.

Sabelko, Rebecca. *Trash to Treasure Crafts*. Minneapolis: Bellwether Media, Inc., 2022.

INTERNET SITES

Brooklyn RobotWorks: Transformers Made of Trash
https://thekidshouldseethis.com/post/transformers-exoskeletons-brooklyn-robotworks

19 Recycled Crafts for Kids
https://www.thesprucecrafts.com/top-trash-to-treasures-crafts-1254258

30 Crafts and Activities Using Upcycled Materials
https://www.weareteachers.com/earth-day-crafts-classroom-activities/

ABOUT THE AUTHORS

Ruthie Van Oosbree

Ruthie is a writer and editor who loves making crafts. In her free time, she enjoys doing word puzzles, reading, and playing the piano. She lives with her husband and three cats in the Twin Cities.

Tamara JM Peterson

Tami grew up tinkering with junk, trying to make something from anything she could dig out of a drawer or out of the woods. Tami lives in Minnesota with her husband, two daughters, and a